natural

INTERIORS

GLOUCESTER MASSACHUSETTS

ROCKPORT PUBLISHERS

Ann McArdle

First published in the United States of America by
Rockport Publishers, Inc.
33 Commercial Street
Gloucester, Massachusetts 01930-5089
Telephone: (978) 282-9590
Facsimile: (978) 283-2742
www.rockpub.com

ISBN 1-56496-609-7

10 9 8 7 6 5 4 3 2 1

Layout: SYP Design & Production

Front Cover Images

Top:	Mark Mack Architects (Photo: Tim Street-Porter)
Bottom Left:	Kalach + Alvarez
Bottom Center:	Gayle Reynolds (Photo: Eric Roth)
Bottom Right:	Winifred Dell'Ario (Photo: Douglas A. Salin)

Back Cover Images

Top:	James Cutler (Photo: Art Grice)
Center:	(Photo: Tim Street-Porter)
Bottom:	Scott Johnson (Photo: Tim Street-Porter)

Printed in China.

contents

introduction   4–5

entrances   6

living rooms   20

dining rooms   44

kitchens   60

bedrooms   76

bathrooms   88

outdoor rooms and patios   100

directory of designers   110

index of designers   112

introduction

With the right materials and colors, you can capture the spirit and beauty of the outdoors in your home. Incorporate the scenery beyond the windows into your home's decor, or—if there's no view—simply evoke the feeling of natural surroundings.

For a home with a panoramic vista, design an interior that mirrors the landscape. In a woodsy area, rough-hewn beams and crude stone surfaces imitate the terrain seen through the windows. In an oceanfront home, create an open-air, beach ambiance by using colors that echo those of the sea and sand.

Where a glimpse of the outside is limited to one's own back yard, the expansive feeling of outdoor space is still attainable. Use like or complementary materials and furnishings for visual continuity between the outdoors and interior. Install a tile floor in a family room that leads out to a tile patio, for instance, for a seamless transition.

Even in the man-made environment of a city, one can capture the essence of the natural world. The key is to use organic materials: Capitalize on the colors and textures of wood grain and stone.

A kitchen equipped with up-to-date appliances can retain a natural quality with wood and stone surfaces for cabinets, floors, and walls. Materials can be rough or smooth, gleaming and light-reflective, or dense and light-absorbing. They can be hard or soft, warm or cool. Use color palettes that imitate nature—dark ochres and browns, rich leafy greens, whites and off-whites, sky and water blues, sunny yellows. The look is unadulterated, free of glitter and frills.

This book shows how noted designers have created natural interiors and offer practical suggestions for maximizing a view and for giving even a closed-off space an outdoor feeling. The woods, mountains, desert, wide-open plains, the sea, and sky can all serve as inspiration. Use the ideas presented in this book to bring the outdoors into your home, combining comfort with raw beauty.

entrances

Give an entryway the feeling of a forest in winter with a wrought-iron balustrade in an angular twig motif.

Photo: Billy Cunningham

Interior Design: Juan Pablo Molyneux

Achieve the look of a grand hacienda with massive, rough-hewn beams. Cool stucco walls work with the warm tones of the wood to make for an inviting entryway.

Photo: Tim Street-Porter

Interior Design: Manolo Mestre

Use terra-cotta floor tiles in an entryway to evoke the feeling of an outdoor patio. Earthenware pots and light-colored natural-wood bookshelves complete the scheme.

Photo: Eric Roth

Interior Design: Gayle Reynolds

Beautify a stairway with a balustrade of finely finished,

varicolored wood.

Photo: © Robert Perron

To set a recreational tone with a touch of whimsy,

construct a balustrade featuring cut-out fish shapes.

White-pigment stain brightens the space without

sacrificing the beauty of the wood grain.

Photo and Architecture: James Cutler

Bring the feel of the forest inside with a balustrade of interwoven twigs.

Photo: Eric Roth

Interior Design: Jill Benedict and Peter Stempel

String halogen lights on wire to illuminate the spaces

between wood beams. The lights also brighten the hall-

way with spots of warmth on the wall and floor. A plaster

sculpture adds a graceful surprise to this rugged setting.

Photo: Art Grice

Architecture: James Cutler

In a contemporary home, use hardwood floors and paneling in transitional spaces such as entryways, hallways, and staircases.

Photo: Tim Street-Porter

Interior Design: Fernau and Hartmann Architects

Mix and match a variety of woods to give an entryway unadorned beauty and a sense of depth. Carefully placed clerestory windows provide plenty of natural light.

Photo: Art Grice

Architecture: James Cutler

Mitigate the rough, heavy appearance of native stone

walls with the sleek, spare lines of contemporary fur-

nishings. Smooth stone floor tiles unite the elements.

Photo: Peter Paige

Interior Design: Tonny Foy

The cooling effect of stucco walls and tile floors in an

entryway can make for a welcome respite from the heat

of the outdoors. An arrangement of flowers and fruit

enlivens the space while echoing the foliage seen

through the window. Large earthenware urns comple-

ment the surrounding textures.

Interior Design: Sistine Interiors

Draw guests into a room through the use of lighting: Illuminate distinctive ceiling detail and light greenery from above. Set floor tiles on a diagonal to point the way, and complete the garden atmosphere with casual wicker armchairs.

Photo: Douglas A. Salin

Interior Design, Lighting, and Architecture: Gordon Stein

Line the wall of an entryway with copper to reflect natural light and create a warm glow. The color and texture of the copper make for a smooth transition between the stone of the floor and the fine wood of the posts and ceiling.

Photo: Michael Lyon

Architecture: Lake/Flato

Soften the boundaries between your living space and the world outside by continuing patio flooring indoors. Architectural details in dark wood unite an interior with its woodsy setting. Make the space more intimate with low, solid furnishings.

Photo: Philip H. Ennis

Design: Frank Lloyd Wright

living rooms

Achieve the look of a cool summer getaway with rough plaster walls painted white and a multitude of windows to let light in. Select pale colors for floor, furniture, and accessories. Complete the mood of the room with tropical plants.

Photo: Carmen Dominguez

Architecture: Enrique Browne

Commune with nature in a sitting room with stone walls, dramatic windows, and a towering ceiling. Stone flooring and Adirondack chairs give the feeling of an outdoor patio even when one is sitting cozily by the fire.

Photo: © Paul Warchol

Interior Design: Marlys Hann

A barn renovation affords the opportunity to create a contemporary home within a historical framework. Leave some rough-hewn beams exposed, and let the original siding show through on the home's interior to link this living space with its working past. Two facing couches flanked by chairs add to the communal feeling of the wide-open, central room. Towering windows provide plenty of light while offering a view of the countryside.

Photo: Richard Bryant/Arcaid

Architecture: Gwathmey Siegel

Build cabinets into the walls of a great-room to house dining ware and conceal clutter. Expansive windows provide light and color from the surrounding landscape.

Photo: Karl Backus

Architecture: James Cutler

A partially broken-away concrete wall can give a room depth and openness. Use pale woods and textured fabrics in stone-like colors to complement architectural materials.

Photo: Karl Backus

Architecture: James Cutler

Give an interior of dark-pine beams, stucco walls, and
slate flooring a hint of warmth with woven rugs in
desert colors. Heavy wood dining furniture and a pale
leather sofa emphasize the contrast of the structural
materials while providing cohesion.

Photo: David Lake

Architecture: Lake/Flato

Make a room feel like a cool desert retreat through the
use of white stone. White floors retain the beauty of the
wood grain when stained rather than painted or carpeted.
Choose accessories in sand tones, and illuminate the
room with wall sconces.

Photo: Dennis Anderson

Lighting Design: Pam Morris

Interior Design: Neal Singer and Bonnie Singer

For a living room that offers a cool respite from hot days and a cozy nest on chilly nights, use soft-hued colors for walls and upholstery. Small windows allow some natural light without letting in too much heat. Wall sconces give evenings a warm glow, enhancing a fire-lit ambiance.

Photo: Kenneth Rice

Lend a feeling of intimacy to a living room with towering ceilings and a stone fireplace-wall through the use of tightly grouped furnishings in rich brown leather and lighter earth tones. Lighten the mood with colorful accent pillows.

Photo: Eric Roth

Interior Design: Edgar Tafel

Exaggerate distinctive architectural features for a unique-looking living room. Balance long windows, a sleek stone fireplace, and horizontal lines with stylized furnishings in earthy tones and natural materials.

Photo: Tim Street-Porter

Interior Design: David Hertz

In an expansive open living area with a view, play off the beauty of immense wood beams and an exposed concrete wall. Unite the elements with a smooth stone floor, and define separate sections with area rugs. Furniture with exposed legs maintains the room's airy feel.

Photo: Tim Street-Porter

Interior Design: Mark Mack Architects

Vaulted ceilings of exposed wood and a window-wall with a panoramic view lend a feeling of openness in any setting. Enhance this expansive effect with lighting from a low-voltage wire system. Unobtrusive details such as low furnishings in earth tones and the simplest of fireplace mantels allow appreciation of the space as a whole.

Photo: Douglas A. Salin

Lighting Design: Linda Ferry

Interior Design: David Allen Smith

Furnish a room with wicker chairs with textured-fabric cushions in earthy tones for a cozy atmosphere. A copper lampshade keeps light from interrupting the fire-lit mood while providing ample illumination for reading.

Photo: Dennis Anderson

Lighting Design: Catherine Ng and Randall Whitehead

Interior Design: Jessica Hall & Associates

Impart a sense of protection from the elements by emphasizing the height and mass of a vaulted ceiling. Draw attention to exposed wood with illumination from sconces mounted on the supporting posts. Align the uprights of built-in shelving with the ceiling joists for a structurally solid impression. Furnish the room in warm, earthy tones to complete the sheltered effect.

Photo: James Benya

Lighting Design: Cynthia Bolton Karasik and James Benya

Interior Design: Gary Hutton

Define the separate areas of an open floor plan with casual furnishings in wicker and solid wood. Use accents of similar color and fabric in each area to visually unify the space. An abundance of natural light completes the inviting atmosphere.

Photo: Luis Poirot

Architecture: Enrique Browne

In an open floor plan lined on both sides with windows, define separate areas with archways. Delineate them further with coordinating area rugs. Dining-room chairs with cane backs maintain the open feeling in harmony with the view through the windows.

Photo: Timothy Hursley
Architecture: Peter Forbes

In a living room with spectacular architecture and an impressive view, keep furnishings simple. Stone-colored upholstery blends with the floor and wall. Use lighting for a decorative effect. Angled wall-washers highlight the detail of the stone, while indirect lighting makes the wood ceiling glow. The etched glass of the tabletop projects a cobbled pattern on the floor when lit from above.

Photo: Douglas A. Salin

Lighting Design: Linda Ferry

Interior Design: Winifred Dell'Ario

Architecture: George Brook-Kothlow

Leave rough-hewn pine beams exposed to add visual warmth to a living room with a stone fireplace and a panoramic woodland view. Use unbleached, textured fabrics on modern furnishings for an appealing, hardy look.

Photo: Tim Street-Porter

Interior Design: Scott Johnson

Use columns to frame a sitting area, making a brick fire-place the room's focal point, for an atmosphere that's at once open and intimate. A profusion of greenery and plenty of natural light bring the outdoors in. Choose earth tones for carpeting and upholstery to add warmth.

Photo and Architecture: Enrique Browne

Line a long row of windows with plants on the inside to blur the distinction between out- and indoors. Here, brick planters complement the tile floor and wood ceiling, creating the backdrop for a lush indoor garden.

Photo and Architecture: Enrique Browne

Retain the look of bare hardwood floors and exposed beams while reaping the benefits of carpeting and comfortable, upholstered furniture. Define a cozy sitting area with a wool rug, and place furniture around its perimeter. Dark tones in the rug draw attention downward, reducing the chilling effect of cathedral ceilings; and neutral upholstery fabrics keep the look fresh.

Photo: Steve Vierra

Partition an open floor plan with built-in wood cabinets.
With accent lighting, the cabinets are a perfect place to
display favorite artifacts. Infuse the space with the feeling of a cozy mountain retreat through the use of wood
and tile floors, warm colors, and a central open fireplace
with a hood.

Photo: Mary Nichols

Lighting Design: Janet Lennox Moyer

Interior Design: Karen Libby

Choose carpet and slipcovers in a stony-gray color to
keep a natural feeling. Emphasize the beauty of
exposed ceiling beams with cabinetry, tables, and doors
crafted from similar kinds of wood.

Photo: © Russell Abraham

Interior Design: Dan Phipps

Blend the desert and the mountains in a rustic living room with dark, rough-hewn beams and contrasting white stucco walls. Add drama with upholstery and rugs in deep, rich tones balanced with white accents and an expanse of shiny hardwood floor.

Interior Design: In-Site Design Group, Inc.

For rustic appeal, use natural wood for floor, ceiling, and end walls, and a sliding barn door to separate rooms from the living space. Functional accents in black, such as a wood-burning stove, a homespun tablecloth, and ceiling fans, add definition while maintaining a unified look.

Photo: Michael W. Cox

Architecture: Gail Lindsey

dining rooms

Give an interior space with an open floor plan a pleasing ambiance with natural light from skylights. The light heightens the warmth of woodwork and plays off a table's stainless-steel accents. Rugs in earth and sky tones provide visual harmony while delineating the room's separate areas.

Photo: Tim Street-Porter

Interior Design: Fernau and Hartmann Architects

Let a brick wall dictate your dining room's decor. Use Venetian-plaster table bases to repeat the color and substance of the wall. Lighten the effect with a glass table-top. A rug with geometric forms complements an angular ceiling and modern chairs, while its colors unify the elements of the room.

Photo: Warren Jagger

Interior Design: Lloy Hack

Use a range of wood tones in an open dining area with sliding glass doors. The darker wood of a table insert pulls together the lighter wood of the table and the reddish tone of the window's framing. Punctuate the space with sleek, black leather chairs to add definition without detracting from the beauty of the wood or of the outdoor scenery.

Photo: © Tom Bonner

Design: Steven Ehrlich

In a dining room with wood paneling, choose a table and chairs that match the wood on the walls for a cohesive effect. Terra-cotta tile floors and open shelving that reveals earthenware pottery complete the natural look.

Photo: © Norman McGrath

Architecture: Alfredo DeVido

For a formal dining room with down-to-earth charm, combine solid, dark furniture with the rough beauty of an exposed wall. Bare, hardwood floors accentuate the room's size, while a tightly centered grouping of table and chairs gives a feeling of intimacy.

Photo: Richard Bryant/Arcaid

Architecture: Gwathmey Siegel

For outdoor appeal in an indoor dining area, install large sliding windows that open the room to the patio and landscape beyond. Use matching flooring inside and out for a seamless transition.

Photo: Karl Backus

Architecture: James Cutler

Use texture and light to create an outdoor feeling in your dining room. Here, polished pine furniture and stone tile floors and wall detail provide a solid, earthy impression. Exterior lighting creates shadow play on the interior wall, while visually extending the boundaries of the room by illuminating the garden outside.

Photo: Dennis Anderson

Interior Design: Jessica Hall & Associates

Lighting Desing: Catherine Ng and Randall Whitehead

Use fine woodwork of white oak to impart warmth to a room with primitive stone walls and floors. Echo the design of a slatted ceiling in the dining-room chairs to provide definition and cohesion.

Photo: Michael Lyon

Architecture: Lake/Flato

Blend inside space with the out-of-doors by continuing your patio's floor treatment in your dining area. Use flame-cut granite pavers to provide cool comfort underfoot. Furnish the room with a simple, solid-wood table lined with wicker armchairs for a casual dining space with an open-air feeling.

Photo: Tim Street-Porter

Interior Design: Richard Meier Architects

Furnish a casual dining area in an oceanfront home with a plain wood table surrounded by mismatched seating with the look of porch furniture. A simple glass bowl of wildflowers echoes the hues of marsh, sea, and sky without shifting the focus from the panoramic view.

Photo: Eric Roth

Set a dramatic tone for your dining room with exterior lighting that illuminates patio plantings. Echo the patio lighting with recessed interior ceiling lights to accentuate surface textures and highlight details. The tile counter and floor and a solid-based, planked-wood table give this room its substantial, earthy feeling.

Photo: www.davidduncanlivingston.com

Lighting and Interior Design: Jeffrey Werner

Create an airy breakfast nook in a windowed corner with
the simplest of furnishings. A sleek-lined banquette
upholstered in textured, earth-toned fabric provides plenty of seating space. Additional chairs reminiscent of tin
watering cans add a casual garden feeling.

Photo: © John Sutton

Interior Design: Dan Phipps and Associates

Bring a tropical air to a casual dining area with a palette
of citrus tones. Cover walls and floors with tiles for a
cooling effect. A terrazzo table and chairs upholstered
in a citrus print unify the colors and secure the motif.

Photo: Peter Margonelli

Interior Design: Piano Nobile

Line an enormous, weathered-pine table with mismatched chairs for a casual dining area. The worn wood gives the room a warmth and density that contrasts with the verdant scene beyond the windows. A jar of sunflowers adds a cheery note.

Photo: Stan Rumbough

Interior Design: Loren Dunlap

Create a cozy sitting area on an enclosed porch with an eclectic mix of cane and upholstered seating. Dress windows with simple bamboo shades to maximize a magnificent mountain view. Add an indoor tree for playful emphasis on the out-of-doors.

Photo: Dave Marlow

Interior Design: Lipkin Warner Design & Planning

kitchens

In a sleek, contemporary kitchen, use earthy floor tiles
and slate countertops. Pale wood tones and stainless-
steel appliances reflect the light from a large window,
creating a bright, energetic ambiance. A built-in shadow
box provides space to display a collection of kitchen
treasures.

Photo: Eric Roth

Interior Design: Michele Foster

Keep the feeling simple in a contemporary kitchen/
dining area with cool stone surfaces. A stark table with
benches provides seating for the whole family without
the added lines of multiple chairs. Lighten the tone of
the room with whimsically designed bar stools in a
warm-colored wood.

Photo: Tim Street-Porter

Interior Design: David Hertz, Syndesis

Mix old and new elements of natural materials to create

the feeling of continuity with the past. Use an aged

exposed post to frame the view of an up-to-date kitchen

outfitted in natural wood and granite. Here, a gleaming

hardwood floor unites the kitchen with the

dining area, which is furnished with a maple table-and-

chairs set from the 1950s. A gridlike balustrade provides

safety without obstructing the view.

Photo: © Rob Karosis

A chunky central island can give a small kitchen a sturdy

feel. Choose solid wood and slate countertops in an

ochre palette to combine utility and style.

Photo: George Ross

Interior Design: Debra A. Blair

Use an array of textures and earth tones to give a small

kitchen with no view a natural feeling. Light reflects off

stone wall tiles, pale granite countertops, and stainless-

steel fixtures to create a warm glow. Thick plank shelv-

ing adds a rugged quality.

Photo: David Hale

Make a sunny kitchen space feel extra cozy with a

window seat cushioned in natural fibers. It's the perfect

setting for relaxed dining or just gazing at the garden

outside. Cool tiles underfoot add balance.

Photo: Bill Rothschild

Interior Design: Shelley Azapian

Add style to a plain, rectangular kitchen by outfitting it with exotic wood cabinetry and a complementary stone countertop, task-lighting fixtures, and a sculptural, stainless-steel range hood.

Photo: © John Sutton

Interior Design: Dan Phipps and Associates

Let a large, stone fireplace set the tone for a cozy kitchen/dining area. A beamed ceiling unites the two spaces. Further coordinate them with a butcher-block dining table that echoes the kitchen's wood island. Use glass-fronted cabinets to balance the heavy wood.

Photo: Story Litchfield

Interior Design: Martin Kuckly

Add a skylight to a kitchen with natural surfaces. Large

terra-cotta floor tiles provide a visually substantial base

for rough pine cabinetry and a brick oven-wall. Granite

countertops reflect light while blending the color and

textures of the other elements.

Photo: Phillip H. Ennis

Interior Design: Rand Elliott

Give a kitchen with classic architecture a rustic feel through the use of rubbed-pine cabinetry and a hardwood floor stained in a checkerboard pattern. Surround the range with a brick wall, and face the range hood with wood to add to the earthy appeal.

Photo: Peter Jaquith

Interior Design: Phyllis D. Greene Interiors

Bring an earthy look to a kitchen with gleaming, stainless-steel appliances by stipple-painting walls in red and copper tones. Add further warmth with pecan countertops. Hang copper pots to visually link the palette to the shiny surfaces.

Photo: Tim Street-Porter

Give an open kitchen a solid presence with a wood-topped island that complements natural-pine coiling beams. Use rush seats for counter stools to add textural definition. A baked-clay tile floor in both the kitchen and adjacent living room unifies the look.

Photo: Tim Street-Porter

Surround a window with tile in varied soft shades of green to frame a leafy view. Hang bundles of drying herbs to erase the boundary between out- and inside. Wood cabinetry and stone countertops in warm tones expand the naturalistic palette.

Photo: John Vaughan

To give a kitchen the appeal of a cabin in the woods, use earth-tone tiles for countertops and floor. Complement exposed, rough-hewn beams with matching paneled walls and cabinetry. Set modern appliances into a mottled brick wall to suggest an open hearth.

Photo: Arch/Balthazar Korab

Emphasize the texture of a wall of rough stone with

light from angled fixtures. Choose wicker chairs with

cushioned seats to visually link the roughness of the

stone with the cozy look of the puffy duvet.

Photo: James Benya

Lighting Design: Cynthia Bolton Karasik and James Benya

Interior Design: Gary Hutton

Achieve a surprisingly airy look in a bedroom with dark,

rough-hewn walls and beams. Furnish it with light, white

furniture. Heighten the effect by choosing bedding in

cool-fabric colors, rugs with a lattice-and-flower pattern,

and delicate porcelain pitchers.

Photo courtesy of Weatherend Estate Furniture

Let skylights brighten a bedroom with exposed ceiling beams. A wide doorway enhances the open, airy feeling.

Photo: Michael W. Cox

Architecture: Gail Lindsey

A red-brick fireplace and hearth enclosure provide warmth and a solid sense of shelter in a bedroom with a window-wall. Position a scatter rug so that it leads the eye to the fire. Dress the bed in light-colored natural fibers to brighten the room while maintaining its organic theme. Add a contemporary lounge chair for contrast.

Photo: Paul Ferrino

Architecture: Peter Forbes

Evoke the American West with a slate-tone floor and solid, rustic furnishings. The wide-open view provides a breathtaking backdrop while counterbalancing the heavy wood and stone interior.

Photo: Bill Timmerman

Interior Design: Stephanie Walters

Stone walls and solid wood cabinets set a tone of simplicity and heartiness. Leather chairs add casual comfort.

Photo: Fabrizio DaRold

Architecture: Marley Porter

Wood walls and floors give a bedroom a country-cabin appeal. Choose simple window treatments and furnishings to keep the focus on the woodsy world outdoors.

Photo: © Norman McGrath

Architecture: Alfredo DeVido

To give a bedroom a tropical look, drape a four-poster bed with mosquito netting. Bamboo wall covering, African-art-inspired accessories, and animal-print pillows complete the effect.

Photo and Interior Design: Myrl Talkington Designs

Outfit a first-floor bedroom with a wall of windows to bring the outdoors in. Where privacy is not an issue, leave the windows bare to show off handsome architectural detail. Use simple, light-colored furnishings oriented toward the windows to enhance the room's wide-open feeling.

Photo: Luis Poirot

Architecture: Enrique Browne

Wood-beamed ceilings can warm a bedroom's concrete walls. A puffy duvet makes the room inviting and restful. To smooth the visual transition from hard surfaces to soft bed, employ a fabric wall-hanging as a headboard. Choose a textile that complements both the color and form of the architectural elements.

Photo: Karl Backus

Architecture: James Cutler

A bold departure from traditional paint schemes can create a surprisingly restful look. Here, the lavender window trim quiets the sandy-yellow tones of the walls and floor. The window acts as a decorative frame for the view.

Photo: Warren Jagger

In a bedroom with a balcony, fashion a sliding door of tight latticework in natural wood. When open, it frames the spectacular view; when closed, it provides light and texture, as well as privacy.

Photo: Luis Gordoa

Design: Kalach + Alvarez

Maximize a bedroom's log-cabin ambiance by furnishing it with an aspen-wood bed and a canopy made from tree branches. Complete the look with a folk-art bedspread.

Photo: Tim Street-Porter

Interior Design: Holly Lueders

bathrooms

Bring the painted desert into your bathroom with tiles of

variegated color and texture.

Photo: Tim Street-Porter

Extend your bathroom into the out-of-doors with an

open-air shower. Surround the shower with canvas

screens for privacy.

Photo: Hickey-Robertson

For a bathroom with rustic appeal, use multicolored

stone tiles for floor and shower, and complement them

with neutral-colored walls and a dark vanity.

Photo: Eric Roth

Interior Design: Gayle Reynolds

Use bamboo as a decorative element in a shower for the feeling of bathing on a tropical island. Handmade tiles in a creamy tone serve as a textural foil for the bamboo, while black accents provide graphic interest.

Photo: Tim Street-Porter

For a bath with a wonderful, cave-like atmosphere, use

heavy materials in deep colors. Plenty of natural light

and yellow tones in the stone keep the space from feel-

ing claustrophobic.

Photo: Tim Street-Porter

For the sensation of bathing in a woodland bower, place your tub beside a long bay of windows. Use pale marble tile and a mirrored wall to reflect both the outside greenery and the potted plants indoors.

Photo: Hickey-Robertson

In a bathroom with a view, use earth tones, natural

wood cabinets, and stone blocks to unite the landscape

and the decor.

Photo: Timothy Hursley

A stone washstand adds the drama of sculpture to a
bathroom. Employ subtle background colors to create
a beautiful stage for this striking element.

Photo: Lourdes Legorreta

Architecture: Victor Legorreta

Approximate the effect of oceanfront scenery with wall-

paper of a shimmering watery blue and a border depicting

a beach scene. Use white stain on bead-board wainscot-

ting to retain the natural wood grain, completing the casual

atmosphere.

Wallpaper by Imperial Wallcoverings

To make a small bathroom seem larger, combine neu-

tral-colored tiling with an open shower stall and tub.

Balance the warm tones of the tiles and ceiling with

walls painted a cool blue.

Photo: Timothy Hursley

outdoor rooms and patios

A wide-open dining space framed with cedar trusses

forms a cathedral-like archway (right) that makes the

most of an exquisite mountain view. Above, a fireplace

built into the exterior wall provides warmth on chilly

evenings.

Photo: www.davidduncanlivingston.com

Architecture: William Turnbull, Jr., and Eric Haesloop

In a temperate climate, incorporate a balcony into your
home's interior. Outfit it with furnishings that are in
keeping with the style of the architecture, such as a
wrought-iron table, wicker chairs, and woven accent
rugs. Terra-cotta floor tiles add color and definition.

Photo: Christopher Covey

Furnish both patio and dining room with picnic bench–style furnishings to afford equal status to interior and exterior spaces. Large windows and glass doors simultaneously separate and unify the two areas.

Photo and Architecture: David Hertz

Complement the cool stone exterior of a sleeping porch

with a rough-timber roof for a tropical feeling. Use

built-in furnishings to keep the look uncluttered.

Complete the motif with a sand-colored futon cover and

a generous scattering of pillows in tribal prints.

Photo: Tim Street-Porter

Design: Gian Franco Brignone

A Mayan room infuses an entryway with dappled natural light. Textured blue walls temper the effect of yellow wood and weighty double doors for an inviting, easy transition from outdoors to in.

Photo: Tim Street-Porter

Design: Manolo Mestre

A breezeway makes for an effortless transition from out- to indoors. Use stone flooring and wood benches to set a rustic tone, and an open grid-work wall for a decorative pattern of light and shadow.

Photo: David Lake

Design: Lake/Flato

Design a patio to enjoy even on chilly nights. Layer meandering vines on a steel-framed trellis for shelter, and add an outdoor fireplace for warmth.

Photo: Grey Crawford

Architecture: Lise Claiborne Matthews

For rustic yet comfortable patio dining, add cotton-covered cushions to rugged timber chairs. The weathered wood of the chairs complements the rough-hewn stone, and an outdoor fireplace provides both warmth and a charming focal point.

Photo: Christopher Covey

Design: John O'Neill and James Palmer

directory of designers

Jill Benedict and Peter Stempel
117 Lexington Road
Lincoln, MA 01773

James Benya
Benya Lighting Design
3491 Cascade Terrace
West Linn, AZ 97068

Debra A. Blair
Blair Design Associates, Inc.
315 West 78th Street
New York, NY 10024

George Brook-Kothlow
George Brook-Kothlow & Associates
P.O. Box AD
Carmel, CA 93921

Enrique Browne
Enrique Browne y Asociados, Arquitectos
Los Conquistadores 2461, Esq. EL
Gobernador
Santiago, CHILE

Zoe Compton
Zoe Murphy Compton, Ltd.
321 Sopris Creek Road
Basalt, CO 81621

James Cutler
135 Parfitt Way S.W.
Balnbridge Island, WA 98110

Winifred Dell'Ario
Design Dell'Ario
P.O. Box 3200
Half Moon Bay, CA 94019

Alfredo DeVido
412 East 85th Street
New York, NY 10028

Loren Dunlap, Artist
P.O. Box 332
Sagaponack, NY 11962

Steven Fhrlich
Steven Ehrlich Architects
10865 Washington Boulevard
Culver City, CA 90232

Rand Elliott, FAIA
Elliott & Associates Architects
35 Harrison Avenue
Oklahoma City, OK 73104

Fernau and Hartmann Architects
2512 Ninth Street
Berkeley, CA 94710

Linda Ferry, IESNA, ASID (affiliate)
Architectural Illumination
P.O. Box 2690
Monterey, CA 93942

Peter Forbes
Peter Forbes and Associates
70 Long Wharf
Boston, MA 02110

Michele Foster
Foster Associates
111 Glen Road
Portsmouth, RI 02871

Phyllis D. Greene Interiors
50 Mill Road
Ipswich, MA 01938

Gustavson/Dundes Architecture and Design
192 Lexington Avenue, Suite 801
New York, NY 10016

Charles Gwathmey, Robert Siegel
Gwathmey Siegel
475 Tenth Avenue
New York, NY 10018

Lloy Hack Associates, Inc.
425 Boylston Street
Boston, MA 02116

Eric Haesloop
Turnbull, Griffin & Haesloop Architects
Pier 1fi, The Embarcadero
San Francisco, CA 94111

Jessica Hall & Associates
1301 6th Street, Suite G
San Francisco, CA 94107-2222

Marlys Hann
52 West 84th Street
New York, NY 10024

David Hertz
Syndesis
2908 Colorado Avenue
Santa Monica, CA 90404

Imperial Wallcoverings
23645 Mercantile Road
Beechwood, OH 44122

In-Site Design Group, Inc.
3551 South Monaco Parkway
Denver, CO 80237

Scott Johnson
Johnson, Fain and Partners, Architects
800 Wilshire Boulevard, 2nd Floor
Los Angeles, CA 90017

Alberto Kalach, Daniel Alvarez
Kalach + Alvarez
Taller Arquitectura
Atlanta 143/3 C.P. 03720
Mexico, D.F.

Cynthia Bolton Karasik
The Lighting Group
200 Pine Street
San Francisco, CA 94109

Martin Kuckly
Kuckly Associates, Inc.
509 East 74th Street
New York, NY 10021

David Lake, Ted Flato
Lake/Flato Architects, Inc.
311 Third Street, Suite 200
San Antonio, TX 78205

Victor Legorreta
Legorreta Arquitectos
Mexico City, Mexico

Gail Lindsey, AIA
Design Harmony
4429 Trommel Court
Wake Forest, NC 27587

Lipkin Warner Design & Planning
P.O. Box 2239
Basalt, CO 81621

Mark Mack Architects
246 First Street
San Francisco, CA 94103

Lise Claiborne Matthews, AIA, ASID
1510 Abbot Kinney Boulevard
Venice, CA 90291

Richard Meier Architects
475 Tenth Avenue
New York, NY 10018

Manolo Mestre
Manolo Mestre Architect
Reforma 2009
Mexico, D.F. 11000

Juan Pablo Molyneux
J.P. Molyneux Studio Ltd.
29 East 69th Street
New York, NY 10021

Pam Morris Designs
Exciting Lighting
14 E. Sir Francis Blvd.
Larkspur, CA 94939

Janet Lennox Moyer, IALD, IES, ASID
6225 Chelton Drive
Oakland, CA 94611

Piano Nobile
233 Aragon Avenue
Coral Gables, Fl 33134

John O'Neill
John O'Neill Architectural Design
508 Mystic Way
Laguna Beach, CA 92651

James Palmer
John O'Neill Architectural Design
508 Mystic Way
Laguna Beach, CA 92651

Dan Phipps and Associates
131 Post Street
San Francisco, CA 94109

Marley Porter
Living Architecture
Austin, TX 78704

Gayle Reynolds, ASID, IIDA
Gayle Reynolds Design
7 Fessenden Way
Lexington, MA 02173

Ann Sacks Tile & Stone
8120 Northeast 33rd Drive
Portland, OR 97211

Sistine Interiors
1359 North Beverly Drive
Beverly Hills, CA 90210

David Allen Smith, Architect
444 Pearl Street, Suite B2
Monterey, CA 93940

Gordon Stein
Stein & Associates
49858 San Juan Avenue
Palm Desert, CA 92260

Edgar Tafel, Architect
14 East 11th Street
New York, NY 10003

Myrl Talkington Designs
6915 Tokalon
Dallas, TX 75214

William Turnbull, Jr.
Turnbull, Griffin & Haesloop Architects
Pier 1fi, The Embarcadero
San Francisco, CA 94111

Stephanie Walters, IIDA, CCIDC
Parisi Interior Design
2002 Jimmy Durante Boulevard., #308
Del Mar, CA 92014

Weatherend Estate Furniture
Imagineering, Inc.
6 Gordon Drive
Rockland, ME 04841

Jeffrey Werner, ASID
Werner Design Associates
35 Yorkshire Lane
Redwood City, CA 94062

Wood-Mode, Inc.
1 Second Street
Kreamer, PA 17833

index of designers

Shelley Azapian 66
Jill Benedict and Peter Stempel 11
James Benya 78
Debra A. Blair 65
Gian Franco Brignone 106
George Brook-Kothlow 37
Enrique Browne 23, 33, 38, 84
Zoe Compton 19
James Cutler 10, 12, 13, 24, 25, 39, 50, 84
Winifred Dell'Ario 37
In-Site Design Group, Inc. 42
Alfredo DeVido 48, 82
Loren Dunlap 59
Steven Ehrlich 48
Rand Elliott, FAIA 70
Fernau and Hartmann Architects 13, 46
Linda Ferry, IESNA 37
Peter Forbes 35, 80
Michele Foster Associates 62
Tonny Foy 14
Phyllis D. Greene Interiors 71
Gustavson/Dundes Architecture and Design 19
Gwathmey Siegel 24, 50
Lloy Hack Associates, Inc. 46
Eric Haesloop 102
Jessica Hall & Associates 32
Marlys Hann 23
David Hertz 29, 52, 105
Gary Hutton 32
Imperial Wallcoverings 98
Scott Johnson 37
Kalach + Alvarez 50, 86
Cynthia Bolton Karasik 98
Martin Kuckly 69
Lake/Flato Architects, Inc. 16, 26, 52, 108
Victor Legorreta 97
Karen Libby 40
Gail Lindsey, AIA 43, 80
Lipkin Warner Design & Planning 59
Holly Lueders 86
Mark Mack Architects 30

Lise Claiborne Matthews, AIA, ASID 108
Richard Meier Architects 52
Manolo Mestre 8, 107
Juan Pablo Molyneux 8
Pam Morris Designs 26
Janet Lennox Moyer, IALD, IES, ASID 40
Piano Nobile 56
John O'Neill 109
James Palmer 109
Dan Phipps and Associates 40, 56, 67
Marley Porter 82
Gayle Reynolds, ASID, IIDA 9, 92
Neal Singer and Bonnie Singer 26
Sistine Interiors 14
David Allen Smith, Architect 30
Gordon Stein 16
Edgar Tafel, Architect 28
Myrl Talkington Designs 83
William Turnbull, Jr. 102
Stephanie Walters, IIDA, CCIDC 81
Weatherend Estate Furniture 78
Jeffrey Werner, ASID 55
Frank Lloyd Wright 17